DESERTS

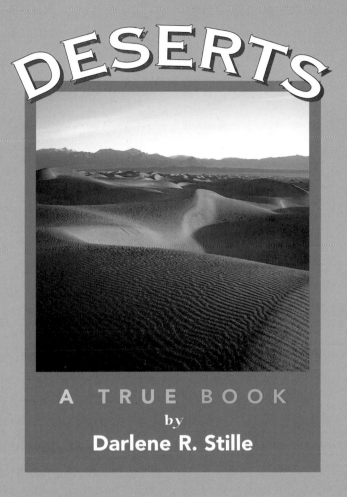

A TRUE BOOK

by

Darlene R. Stille

Children's Press®

A Division of Grolier Publishing

New York London Hong Kong Sydney
Danbury, Connecticut

Monument Valley, Utah

Reading Consultant
Linda Cornwell
*Coordinator of School Quality
and Professional Improvement
Indiana State Teachers
Association*

Content Consultant
Jan Jenner, Ph.D.

Author's Dedication
*For Cynthia A. Marquard,
who showed me some of the
world's great ecosystems*

*The photo on the cover
shows an area of the Sonora
Desert in Arizona. The photo
on the title page shows sand
dunes in Death Valley
National Park in California.*

**Visit Children's Press® on the
Internet at:
http://publishing.grolier.com**

Library of Congress Cataloging-in-Publication Data

Stille, Darlene R.
    Deserts / by Darlene R. Stille.
        p.   cm. — (A True book)
    Includes bibliographical references and index.
    Summary: Presents a general description of deserts and describes spe-
cific desert plants, animals, people, and activities.
    ISBN 0-516-21508-6 (lib.bdg.)   0-516-26760-4 (pbk.)
    1. Deserts—Juvenile literature.   [1. Deserts.] I. Title. II. Series.
GB611.S75   1999
551.41'5—dc21   98-53856
                                                                    CIP
                                                                    AC

© 1999 Children's Press®
a Division of Grolier Publishing Co., Inc.
All rights reserved. Published simultaneously in Canada.
Printed in the United States of America.

GROLIER
PUBLISHING   1 2 3 4 5 6 7 8 9 10 R 08 07 06 05 04 03 02 01 00 99

Contents

What Is a Desert? 5

Desert Plants and Animals 9

The World's Largest Desert 19

The World's Coldest Deserts 26

Farming in the Desert 29

Mining in the Desert 32

People of the Desert 36

To Find Out More 44

Important Words 46

Index 47

Meet the Author 48

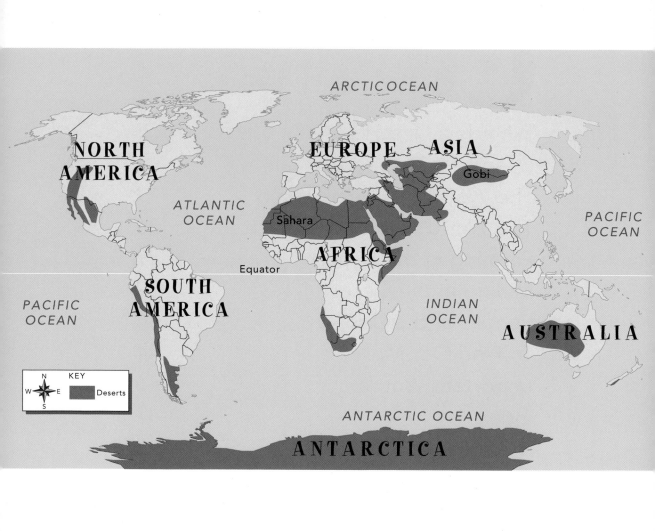

What Is a Desert?

Is a desert a hot place with nothing but sand? A few deserts are like this. But most are not.

You may be surprised to learn that some deserts are very cold. So what exactly is a desert? A desert is a place that is very dry because it gets very little rain.

If you visited a desert in the Middle East, you might see waves of sand. The wind blows the sand into huge piles called dunes.

Desert sands come in many colors. This red sand desert is in Saudi Arabia.

Mesas are a common site in Canyonlands National Park in Utah.

If you visited a desert in the southwestern United States, you would see that the ground is covered with small stones and sand. There are gigantic rocks that look like huge tables. These rocks are called mesas.

A variety of
cactuses and
wildflowers
grow in the
Sonora Desert
in Arizona.

Desert Plants and Animals

Some kinds of plants can live on desert land. Wildflowers, cactuses, trees, and shrubs all grow in deserts in the south-western United States.

These plants have special features that help them get water. Some have very long roots that can reach water deep under the ground. Others are able to store water from desert rainstorms.

Cactuses are the best-known desert plants. All cactuses have sharp spines that protect them from animals. There are many

Some cactuses are small and have brightly colored flowers.

The giant saguaro cactus has one large root that grows straight down and many smaller roots that fan out to collect rainwater.

kinds of cactuses. Some are small, and some are large. The largest cactus is the giant saguaro. It has a tall, thick trunk with branches that look like raised arms.

These date palms are growing in an area of the Egyptian desert that is close to the Nile River.

Very few plants grow in the deserts of Africa and the Middle East. Date palms grow in places where they can get enough water.

Many different kinds of
animals live in deserts.
During the day, you might
see insects, snakes, and
lizards. At night, you might

This western diamondback rattlesnake
hides near a cactus in Arizona.

hear the howl of a coyote or the hoot of an owl.

Most deserts are very hot during the summer, so some desert animals spend their

days in cool underground bur-
rows. They come out at night to
look for food. This is how kanga-
roo rats, centipedes, scorpions,
and rattlesnakes survive.

A giant desert centipede

The black tailed jackrabbit lives in desert areas of North America.

Other desert animals have special features that help them stay cool. Many lizards and insects are light colored. Their bodies reflect sunlight and heat. Desert foxes and rabbits can keep cool because they lose heat through their long ears.

Larger animals, such as mule deer, bobcats, and coyotes come to the desert to look for food after it rains. The best-known large desert animal is the camel.

Camels live in the deserts of Africa and the Middle East. They can go for days without drinking water. They store fat in their humps and use the fat for energy when there is no food.

A group of nomads rides camels through a desert area in Jordan.

Because a camel can carry people and goods across miles of sand, it is called "the ship of the desert."

The World's Largest Desert

Imagine a desert as big as the United States. That's the size of the Sahara, the world's largest desert. It covers parts of nine countries in northern Africa.

There are mountains in some parts of the Sahara. Other parts are gravel-covered plains,

The Sahara is the largest desert in the world. Can you imagine what it would be like to get lost there?

but much of the Sahara is made of sand.

The Sahara is very hot during the day, so only a few plants and animals can live there. Some plants sprout after a rainfall and live for only a few weeks. The seeds they produce lie in the ground until the next rainfall.

Very few plants can survive the harsh conditions of the Sahara.

Fennec foxes can survive in the desert because they lose heat through their big ears.

A few large wild animals live in parts of the Sahara. There are foxes, sheep, a type of antelope called the

Wild sheep live on the northern edge of the Sahara.

addax, and a type of gerbil. Snakes and lizards also live in this huge desert.

An oasis is an area in a desert where there is enough water for plants to grow. When people cross the Sahara, they stop at oases to rest and water their animals.

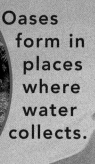

Oases form in places where water collects.

an Oasis?

Sometimes the water at an oasis bubbles up from a spring. Sometimes people reach underground water by digging wells. The banks of a desert river can also be an oasis.

An oasis can be very small, or it can be very big. A large oasis in Asia called Merv is as big as the state of Delaware.

This oasis in Peru is a welcome sight for people traveling across the desert.

The World's Coldest Deserts

The Gobi is the largest dry, cold desert in the world. It is twice as big as the state of Texas. The Gobi is in an Asian country called Mongolia.

Some scientists think of Antarctica as a desert. Antarctica is a large continent

Bactrian camels can survive in the harshest deserts. This camel is in the middle of the Gobi.

that surrounds the South Pole. Antarctica is not a dry desert, however. There is plenty of fresh water, but it is almost always frozen as ice or

There is no liquid fresh water in Antarctica, so many scientists think of it as a desert.

snow. Because there is no liquid fresh water in Antarctica,
very few plants or animals can
live there.

Farming in the Desert

Desert land is dry, but if people water it enough, they can grow crops there. The water may come from a spring or a well in an oasis. It may also come from canals that carry water from rivers.

Bringing water from a river to farmland is called irrigation.

A canal runs through a grove of orange trees in California (left). These sunflowers (below) would die if the land they grow on was not irrigated.

Sometimes the water fills little ditches beside each row of plants. Sometimes the water is sprayed all over the field with big sprinklers.

Farmers spray water over these bean plants to help them grow. The land they grow on used to be a desert.

Irrigation has helped people turn some deserts into farms. The Imperial Valley in California was once a desert. Today, farms there grow crops all year round.

Mining in the Desert

Metals and minerals are often found in desert rocks and soil. Rocks and soil that hold metals or minerals are called ore.

People have found gold, silver, lead, copper, and uranium ore in deserts. They have also found oil and gas

A huge copper mine in Arizona

Ghost towns are common in the southwestern United States. The buildings shown in this picture are part of Bodie, California. Bodie was abandoned many years ago.

in deserts. Much of the world's copper comes from mines in Arizona deserts.

People set up mines in deserts to dig out the ore. Sometimes towns grow up around the mines. When the ore is all gone, the mines close and people move away from the towns. These empty towns are called ghost towns. There are many ghost towns in the southwestern United States.

People of the Desert

Long ago, people learned to live in deserts. In Africa and the Middle East, some people built houses around oases. Other people moved from place to place with their animals. They were called shepherds.

A group of shepherds called the Bedouins still live in the

A group of shepherds has set up a camp in the desert of Saudi Arabia.

A Bedouin man
with his camel

Sahara. They wear long robes
and live in tents. The Bedouins
move from place to place look-
ing for water and food for their
camels, goats, and sheep.

People also learned to travel across deserts many years ago. They used camels to carry cloth, animal skins, and other goods to trade. They traveled across the Sahara in long lines called caravans.

A caravan of camels moves slowly across the Sahara.

Sandstorms

Wind on a desert blows sand around. A strong wind can cause a sandstorm. Sometimes there is so much sand in the air that people cannot see. They find it hard to breathe.

Sometimes a strong sandstorm forms a dust devil. A dust devil looks like a whirling pillar of sand moving across the desert.

Native Americans learned
to live in the deserts in the
southwestern United States.
They used a type of mud
called adobe to build houses
called pueblos. The pueblos

Native Americans built
these pueblos in the
New Mexico desert.

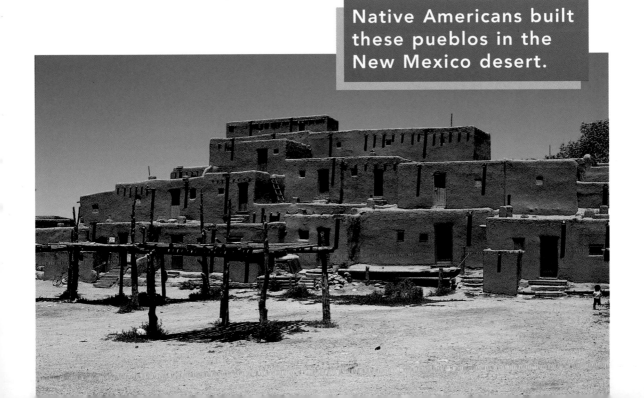

were stacked on top of one another, so they looked like apartment buildings.

Today, millions of people live on desert land. Phoenix and Tucson in Arizona are both built in the southwestern desert. The people who live in these cities know that water is the secret to life in the desert. They get the water they need from canals connected to the Colorado River.

The city of Tucson,
Arizona, was built in the
middle of the desert.

To Find Out More

Here are some additional resources to help you learn more about deserts:

 **Books**

Inserra, Rose and Susan Powell. **The Kalahari.** Heinemann, 1997.

Lambert, David. **People of the Deserts.** Raintree Steck-Vaughn, 1998.

Lesser, Carolyn. **Storm on the Desert.** Harcourt Brace, 1997.

Pipes, Rose. **Hot Deserts.** Raintree Steck-Vaughn, 1998.

Ruth, Maria M. **The Deserts of the Southwest,** Marshall Cavendish, 1998.

Savage, Stephen. **Animals of the Desert.** Raintree Steck-Vaughn, 1997.

Organizations and Online Sites

Desert Ecosystem

http://www.npr.org/ programs/sfkids/showarchive /sfkc.97.11.14.html

A presentation by National Public Radio that includes audio files, questions and activities for students, and other reference resources.

Desert Life in the American Southwest

http://www.desertusa.com/ life.html

Learn all about the environment, plants, animals, and people of the southwestern deserts.

Sahara Desert Field Study Centre

http://www.gibnet.gi/ ~stdavids/sahara/home .htm

Good pictures of life in the Sahara, especially date-palm farming.

Important Words

adobe a type of mud used by Native Americans to build homes in the desert

cactus a desert plant with sharp spines that protect it from animals

dune a hill of sand

irrigation bringing water to farmland by filling little ditches beside each row of plants or by spraying water on the field with big sprinklers

mesas rocks that look like huge tables

oasis a place in the desert where there is water

ore rocks and soil that hold metal or minerals

pueblos Native American homes made of adobe

sandstorm a storm in the desert caused by strong winds that blow sand around

46

Index

(**Boldface** page numbers indicate illustrations.)

adobe, 41, 46
animals, 9, 13–18, **16,** 20, **22, 23,** 28, 38
Antarctica, 26–28, **28**
Bedouins, 36–38, **38**
cactus, **8,** 9–11, **10, 11,** 13, 46
camel, 17–18, **18,** 27, 38–39, **38, 39**
canal, 29, **30,** 42
caravans, 39, **39**
desert, defined, 5
dunes, 1, 6, 46
farming, 29–31, 46
Gobi Desert, 26, **27**
ghost towns, **34,** 35
Imperial Valley, 31
insects, 13, 15, **15,** 16

irrigation, 29, **30,** 31, 46
lizards, 13, 16, 23
mesas, 7, **7,** 46
mining, 32–37
national parks, **1, 2, 7**
Native Americans, 41, **41,** 46
oasis, 24–25, **24, 25,** 29, 36, 46
ore, 32, **33,** 35, 46
plants, **8,** 9–12, 20–21, **21,** 24, 28, 30–31, **31,** 46
pueblo, 41–42, **41,** 46
rainfall, 5, 10, **11,** 21
Sahara, 19–20, **20, 21,** 22, **23,** 24, 38, 39, **39**
sandstorm, 40, 46
snakes, 13, **13,** 15, 23
Sonora Desert, **1, 8**
water, 9, 12, 17, 24, **24,** 27–30, **28, 31,** 42, 46

Meet the Author

Darlene R. Stille lives in Chicago, Illinois, and is executive editor of the World Book Annuals and World Book's Online Service. She has written many books for Children's Press, including *Extraordinary Women Scientists*, *Extraordinary Women of Medicine*, four True Books about the human body, and four other True Books about ecosystems.